Healing Strategies

For Women at War

•

seven black women poets

Healing Strategies
For Women at War

crocus

Healing Strategies
For Women at War
seven black women poets

First published by Crocus in 1999

Crocus Books are published by
Commonword Limited
Cheetwood House, 21 Newton Street,
Manchester. M1 1FZ.

Printed by Printflow Colour Limited,
2-4 Moor Lane, Bolton. BL1 4TH.

Cover design by Verso Design Ltd,
Rutland House, 18 Hilton Street, Manchester. M1 1FR.

Crocus Books are distributed by Turnaround Ltd,
Unit 3, Olympia Trading Estate, London. N22 6TZ.

Commonword gratefully acknowledges financial assistance from
the Association of Greater Manchester Authorities, North West
Arts Board and Manchester City Council.
Commonword expresses special acknowledgement of financial
support for this book from Yorkshire and Humberside Arts Board.

British Library Cataloguing-in-Publication Data. A catalogue
record for this is available from the British Library.

Contents

Maya Chowdhry

Marie Guise Williams

SuAndi

Shamshad Khan

Trudy Blake

Tang Lin

Seni Seneviratne

Introduction

The poems in this collection are part of a significant trend; they contribute to a growing body of work that can be perceived not only as postcolonial literature but more specifically, as Black British literature.

During the last ten years or more, new voices have been emerging: those of men and women of African or Asian descent who were either born in Britain or came here as young children in the fifties, sixties and seventies. The acknowledgement of these poets, novelists and dramatists has been painfully slow; the media has consistently ignored Black British writers in favour of African-Americans. Few mainstream publishing houses have supported such literature; instead, it has fallen to community publishers such as Crocus to enable such voices to be heard.

This collection of poems gives voice to the diversity of first and second generation experiences of living in Britain. The writers' origins are as varied as the poems themselves and encompass regions such as Sri Lanka, India, Pakistan, China and the Caribbean. All the poets are women, who represent the double challenge and struggle implicit in being Black and female. One of the main issues is that of identity, and this engenders explorations of displacement, sexuality, mother-daughter relationships and the need to transcend stereotypical constructions of race and gender. These explorations occur both at a thematic level and at a formal one; the poems constantly push the boundaries of language and refuse the conventions of standard English. They are hybrids, born out of the many cultural influences that have shaped the experiences of these writers. And they are poems, for the most part, which have come out of the oral tradition and which are therefore often written to be shared through performance, as well as living on the page. The strength of this collection is its diversity, and indeed, diversity is celebrated here and is implicitly presented as our hope for the future.

Being Black *and* British in these poems frequently forms an integral part of the work. Consequently, British identity emerges as being at least as significant as the other cultural identities assumed by these writers. This marks a shift in Black writing in this country, which in the past has often represented British identity as being secondary or non-existent. However, although many common themes are represented by these poets, each articulation is different and points to the richness of the multi-culturalism that is now an aspect of British life.

Healing Strategies For Women at War must be read by all those who have an interest in postcolonial, Black British writings. It is hoped that it marks a period in which such writing is nurtured and given the recognition that it needs in order to flourish.

Jacqueline Roy
Senior Lecturer in Post Colonial and Creative Writing, Manchester Metropolitan University.

Foreword

There are too few women of colour poets published in England and then only sparingly within anthologies. The seven women in this collection, all based in the North of England, have already established their reputations regionally. This collection contains a sufficient body of innovative work to place them on the national poetry map.

Women from across age and colour divides will be drawn to these writings. There are poems recalling childhood and adolescence, such as Marie Guise Williams' *My Mother's Old Coat #3*, and *In Love With Mr Gibson*; other poems are humorous, like Trudy Blake's and SuAndi's bittersweet stories of relationships. Seni Seneviratne neatly pulls the drawstrings together to tell stories of first and subsequent generations living in England. The cultural echoes in Shamshad Khan's *Silver Threads* provide enhanced colour and distinct flavour, while Tang Lin fuses traditional Chinese writing forms with modern settings and concerns, and Maya Chowdhry, in the title poem, *Healing Strategies for Women at War* neatly encompasses the way in which so many women are forced to live.

The poets all demonstrate that their various cultural backgrounds are an essential part of their writing, adeptly combining the experiences of living in England with the contradictions it so often forces us to live. They depict the fight and frustrations we continually find ourselves in, how we struggle to make sense of it all in order to retain our sanity in a country that decides, whenever it wants to, that it is our host and not our home.

These women offer up 'healing strategies', and are we not always at war? - women of colour, fighting for our recognition, to be treated as people of worth instead of second class citizens.

Kadija Sesay
Poet.

Editors' Note

When we invited initial contributions we had no idea what sort of anthology would result. Only that the work of lesser known black women writers remained largely unpublished by mainstream writers. Also, as editors, we wanted to create an anthology of work which reflected our experiences as women living within a multiplicity of cultures. Here are seven women writers, each writing with a distinct voice, whose inspiration ranges from coats and photographs, disfigured hearts and familial relationships, to clifftop love trysts and a woman's physical discourse with her own body.

We sought to share intimately these things, so it was consciously decided that *Healing Strategies* should have more than just a smatter of poems by each woman. Each poet is given enough space to do justice to her own poetic voice; each reader enough scope to find something of particular personal resonance. We hope the book meets our initial aim of bringing very distinct, fresh writing to the eyes of those who seek to enjoy it.

It has been a pleasure working with our sister poets, seeing our vision come to fruition. However, we recognise that there is room for many more collections and hope that other black women, and women in general, are inspired to translate their own voices into print. In this way much of the dynamic work which is often witnessed in performance can be indelibly recorded in the making of a new, inclusive contemporary history.

We would like to thank, Cultureword, Crocus Books and the many people who helped us see this Project through to the end. A special thanks to Pete Kalu of Cultureword who has lent his skill and support from the outset.

Marie, Lin, Shamshad

Maya Chowdhry

As a teenager poetry was my lifeline. Now it's an occupation (dangerous?). My poems have been published in *Putting In The Pickle Where The Jam Should Be* and numerous anthologies including *As Girls Could Boast*.

I won the 1992 Cardiff International Poetry Competition with *Brides of Dust*. My first radio play *Monsoon*, was a winner in the 1991 BBC Radio Young Playwrights Festival. In the last seven years, I have written five radio plays and five plays for stage, of which *Monsoon, Four Corners, An Appetite for Living* and *Splinters* use the poetic form. I am currently working on a collection of poetry : *The Seas of Neptune.*

Healing Strategies for Women at War

one: leave knives on the chopping board.
two: fry your love in hot oil
until it reaches flash point.
three: stir yourself up
with therapy books on anger, pinch yourself
to see if you're still alive.
four: lay the table with friends,
placing them carefully, separate with
napkins, knives, forks and spoons.
five: cut yourself into thin slices.
six: bake your dreams until
they carbonize in the oven.
seven: stew family photographs. remember,
comparisons and memories should be kept secret.
eight: feed your addictions with the guilt of
using broken biscuits as a base for your life.
nine: sprinkle (don't talk don't trust don't feel)
into conversations about happiness.
ten: devour the emotional distress
and wounds of others
as your mirror.
eleven: boil yourself in the pain of leaving
every time someone falls in love with you.
twelve: ferment ginger wine kisses
until they burn your lips.
thirteen: use pancakes garnished with
chillies to stuff your feelings into.
fourteen: sift your desires through others' needs.

fifteen: ice sex with pink fondant
and lie about what you want.
sixteen: eat lotus root filled with miso
and pretend you're healthy.
seventeen: make yourself
a packed lunch and leave home.

identity song

there are city signs
around and the motorway
arrows don't give me
no home-coming welcome
here on holiday?
no just living.

a woman on the bus
with a mixed race kid
swears she's white
her thick black hair
and masala skin defy her mother
pretends she hasn't
noticed
that the other kids at school
call her curry face
throw chillies in her eyes.

you buy your jeans from
Southall market and
say you won't ever go out with
no paki boys don't want them
touching your charcoal hair,
say you won't marry no
crimson powder parting on your head
and your black bindi means anarchy.

my grandmother has an X
in her passport means
she won't tell me
no hand-me-down tales
for me and my grandchildren
if the phone line
ever connected she'd
say stolen land
and now they've stolen
you from me.

the seamstress

she looks up
the needle swaying
under the weight of the words
red thread scratching the
outer seams of a silk kameez

she can't recognise your
almond eyes dripping onto the cloth,
your body has changed,
become distorted,
your tawny skin seems
different because it has lain
under a woman's hand

she thinks luckily she's
already measured your
breasts, your hips, your
inside leg, because now
she doesn't want to put
her tape measured hand there

it's no longer
a woman's inside thigh
the measurement has
expanded,
become an unknown domain
a terrifying territory

and now your clothes
are one size larger,
the cloth hanging wide around
your breasts
your inside thigh,
and your salwaar is so
tight around your ankle
you can hardly get them on

Indian Ocean

The sea travels from
Mandvi to Ganga Sagar knows
no cease-fire
line or the difference
between a European and an Indian
body, except the sea
knows me, my brown skin
travels from Mandvi
to Ganga Sagar unravelling
around the coasts of India
travelling from
the Arabian Sea to the Bay
of Bengal the sea travels across
oceans and does not know that one
country has ended and another begun
that the spices in Sainsburys
travel
that the silk in Libertys travels
that people travel
except the sea
finds their bodies
on her ocean bed
and unpicks their flesh until
they are bones
and only the sea knows where
she has hidden them

Measured and Microwaved

She has
old fashioned soap, a jar of biscotti, M&S coffee,
Greek magazines amongst quiet taste
and a sense of organisation verging
on too methodical. She likes to
fuck journalists and critics, use at least three fingers
and her best hand. She serves them
microwaved pasta on green plates,
and points out the page number
in her recipe book. She says
she's memorised all the recipes so
she has more time to write.

She reads the *Merchant of Venice*
perched on her balcony overlooking
red brick and other balconies.
It's small and anonymous
and you can loose yourself in
the calm light of the sky. She leaves her
watch on the desk so she can sleep white
sheet dreams and return to measure the seconds her
words take to draft. She wonders if it's possible
to cycle to the bagel shop before
her first scene is written, before she's lived
the first act, before her sleepless nights
close around her and make her forget.

She wants to buy small blue fishes to dart around
the edges of her bath, a green tea-towel to match
the plates, an ice-maker
to chill her passionate nights without skin.
She wants to remember. Everything in the fridge
has its own shelf, its own
elastic band snapping into place, keeping
out cold and dryness,
keeping in
places to return to.

Stretches of For-get-me-knots

Behind your step
is a moment waiting
for fortune undulating
into hazy places
where you unzip small breaths
along a narrow path
with the jagged angle
of your elbow to the sky
and tongue to belly in dusk's light
the taste disappearing
into islands which wash upon
their own shore
the weathered passion
of expectation.

Below your knee
I see a hand searching
a rhythm beginning,
a wish saturated.
after it begins I kiss the cliff edge
knowing there are no lies
in desire
no half measures in willing
no places to leave undone.

I lay open
tied by for-get-me-knots
and green
my fingers tear at clumps
your fist breaks into a palm
as you swim into whispers
sharp as the cliff edge
hanging hard and hot into
fenced reminders of how sand
was once rock.

The sky yawns into dusk
blows fragments of your rapture
into legs snaked in embrace
I lie spread
a picture of plenty
a box unwrapped
and look where there is a whole stretch
of the cliff path to be walked.

red wine

she eats holly berries and watches
the midnight TV flicker, reaching for
crushed velvet to bring her
tongue alive, keep the tears inside.

she sings Christmas carols in June,
thinks of grapes fizzing in the sun,
her bare feet on sour red lino stinging
falling into brown paper and dust.

she swims for hours,
grapeskins in her ears,
takes a ruby aperitif and lies
to you about promises.

she drowns in crimson dye, choking on
pain and wanting irony
tastes like cheap vinegar
cochineal laughter burning her mouth.

she washes her hair in rosemary, plaits it,
winding the strands tight,
grows roses and years, becomes
fat and empty and forgotten.

the one-colour-only countries

make religious labels
to die for and red soil
is replaced with family sand.

my grandmother never knew her
mother was sikh/hindu prayers
give me my name
and leaves fall the same in
both countries.

O.S.

The sky is sculpted
into brickwork sunsets
glass horizons
and a new place to see
the city from

You
sent
me an ordinance survey
map so I could find the
steep contours of your language. I looked
all day
in the library trying
to find those places,
maybe it wasn't even England.

The day-trippers
I keep meeting
all morning tell me
there's no A-Z
for this town

I
walk
up and down
a one-way street looking
for a way out

Alfred Khan

A rat scratches,
swims a breadth
through canal slime,
nail varnish slips from
moist fingers
a spilt omen on blue chiffon.
Damn the dress's ruined.

Miss Mexicana, your
five minute call.

Squealing back.
My nerves are shattered.
Tugging on lime green
lurex replacement,
not worn since
the Kevin days
or was it Brian
and white lilies?

One minute
is called.

I said shattered!

Shave the last remnants,
push size eights

into gold stilettos,
powder on fake cleavage,
lips outlined.
I want to be all woman.

Gloria's introduction
lyrics swimming harder
than rats.

I will survive.

HIV-1-discordant

she drinks wide
fractured and purple
her lips bleed forgetting
she sucks into
the desire beyond
chance

she says the rust
on the needle stung
her, seasoned and gleaming
translating the **r** of risk
into the **r** of reason

her wrists wear rope burns
hands blue nails
woman to woman
she splits your skin
laughs at what
you'll both enjoy
sharing, snips you
scissors you, until
you're frightened of her
mouth, tongue, lips, hair
until you can't
stand to touch
the broken places
you thought
you could avenge

she drinks
you take
the risk

Cruising on line

JANET said an old flame
picked her up
internet.
I say burn in hell
you wanna start a war with
all your C-U-SEE-ME
chat up lines.

VERONICA says get on line,
dial her up anytime,
send her love poems TCP,
and if you have to relay
her internet chat
then don't repeat the gossip.
Says if you wanna have
sex on the net
better get a 32 bis
and gopher yourself from Miami to Berlin.

Says she breathes telnet when she comes
wants you to lick every bit of her
and spread your WAIS
in her direction
give her vibrations beyond the world wide web.

JANET says every
last flame was a Usenet junkie
spilt her love
in rivers of dumped digital harmonies
AND SHOUTED BACK AT HER.

Now she wants some internet newbie to share her
shareware days and nights
says she ended
her last relationship with a cancelbot
and developed kill
files to stop the love
waves
transatlantic
waves from reaching her.

Celtic Knots

she takes the thread
i listen to belonging
makhan
zamin
ghar
between her fingers
three times
come
listen
touch
i swim in breath
and rest my fingers
in her lips
three times
pani
samudr
hava
she ties the thread
three times
wide
hand
after
around my wrist
my fingers slip
into
her
mouth

into the knot
she sucks
wet
skin
open
the thread lies
between
my
skin
and
hers

Marie Guise Williams

I have been writing for eight years now. My poetry and short fiction have been published in anthologies including *Dancing on Diamonds*, *Nailing Colours* (Crocus), *Stranger at my Table* (Women's Press), and in various small magazines. My writing is cathartic and seeks to explore the effects of my repressed Christian childhood, as well as less obvious influences on my culture, sexuality and gender. I try to approach these subjects with integrity and eloquence, and hope others can identify with the results.

An Ode To Two Junes

(For June Jordan and June Marie Evans)

The only reason I'd keep the name I was born with
is because it also belongs to you.
June.
When I say it and see your picture
or remember your long-skirted figure
on the platform those two times
I see apple blossoms and sweet potato pudding
and the year's first hot day
notwithstanding the day my poetry muse returned.
I remember that one awkward kiss
that inadequate thanks to you from me,
after all a stranger, clutching your publicity brochure
trying to share with you my earnest gratitude
from the long tunnel of anonymity
at the other end of your autograph.

June.
Different again the imprint of your face.
And how strange to be able to say it
and not have to remember one picky-headed girl,
snotty-nosed and wearing trainers with floral dress
under a duffel coat and the obligatory bobble hat.
Whose only words of paternal recognition
likened her to a son.
Who stood alone against that cruel, cruel
        presumption
that girls must have long hair, pretty hairpins.

Manhead! Instantly mistaken for a boy;
no girlie affectations yet to prove them wrong
no real sexuality yet to see myself right—
awkward with no hips at the top of those thighs
and yet, still running anyway.

In Love with Mr Gibson

I am ten years old and in the back of his car.
It is after school
and we are on the way to inter-school athletics,
but he has brought his wife along
which makes me 'the other woman'.

Doesn't she know
how we make love with our eyes
in the classroom?
How the bow in his legs, his calves
belong to me?
How can I explain
how when he marks my News and Story book
he shares his cologne with me,
ushering me into a secret place we inhabit
of which we have never spoken openly
of which I could never tell my friends?
Didn't she see the way he was searching
for my eyes in the rear view mirror?
How he will speak gently to me when
he tells me to *shut up and get changed*,
to let me know how sorry he is
that I must go through this humiliation alone?

We are in love,
and the fact that my desk
is in front of the blackboard
is no accident. It can't be.

Nor how he reads my stories aloud in class
commenting on how good certain bits are,
dishing out extra praise with direct eye contact,
crossing his legs as he leans back in the chair
as though it is a hot summer's night
and he is bathed in the aura of my love letters.
Mr Gibson loves me,
and this woman - his so called wife -
the one who uses his surname,
who expects the privilege
of the front passenger seat in his car
could never understand all this.
There is love between the lines
as we discuss the introduction of the twenty pence
        piece,
though it appears on the surface
to be a three way conversation.
But she will never know about this
and I guess I should feel bad.

But I don't.
I think this even as I see how beautiful she is,
as I make harsh laser cut outs in the back of her seat,
feeling beneath for some hidden ejector button
to get her out of his life.
Yet, although she shares breakfast with Mr Gibson,
his car and his address,
I have his intimate emotional secrets,
eight gold merits,
his bow legs
and his calves.

The Doorstep

Darren was this white guy
from when I was
fascinated with rock music

who looked incredibly like Mick Jagger
and told me
I kissed like a vacuum cleaner

who once walked me home
all the way from the Banshee
balancing his cycle in one hand
and my hand in his other

I wonder
what we must have talked about
3am Friday
hungover and in Hulme?

but
before I knew it
he was leading me into the alley
down one side of our terrace

having his mouth treated
with my special suction action
gasping for air
as he came back for more

then nodding *hello*,
as he strolled away home,

to my elder sister
who was waiting mortified
in our doorway

Parallels

I

My father.
A selfish old man
feigning penitence
only just recalling
the place where
the axe
    fell
where he planted
his seed.
That seed
being threefold.
Perhaps why
the humble helpless act
he performs now
fools only himself.
I remember only
a cussing man
parading the house
displaying his power;
the sweat-grimed towel
swathing his left shoulder
One side was always free
so with flick
of wrist
his belt could
be easily undone.

II

When you collapsed
on top of me
post orgasm
you reminded me of
that boy
the day
he kicked me in
the doorway
until I thought
    my periods
      had begun.
For a second
your wet body repelled
me. I wanted to
push you off me
like I would a rapist.
You never wondered,
stopped to think.
You took my sacrifice
and disappeared into
the night. Leaving me
with nothing
to hold onto, but
sweat-grimed sheets -
something which cannot
be easily undone.

My Mother's Old Coat #3

My mother has several of these
which she makes me try on
each time I go there
hoping I will fit into her old self
and take it places she has never been:
through the gates of divorce
and into new territory.
She tries to sell me the antiques of her soul
in tweed and polyester and fabrics I don't recognise
and I place them down discreetly
as quietly I leave
in a guise of my own.

Love Comes Calling

I love it when
love comes calling
falling anonymously
like snow amongst rain
so for a moment
we might see it differently
and then perhaps
not at all

or like hail
hitting hard
on each nerve-ending
love stings the fingers delicately
pricks the conscience privately
perhaps not so much
warming the soul
as making it aware
of the changing of seasons.

The Transformation Place

They arranged themselves into beautiful
patterns shapes movements   no boundaries
first on top of the Indian duvet, then
slowly climbing downward and inside
amidst the underness.
He touched the inside of where she felt burnt out
substituted love in every place
where pain had lodged too long.

When night came it was wet and shiny
creamy and liquid, foaming around their secret room.
After the coming she rolled in the wet spot
took him in her arms and to a place beyond sleep
beyond dreams.
When he was satisfied, she now hungry
they rearranged again. He became her spoon -
lick him and he would stick.

In the morning they slowly counted 10
separated into 9 to 5, and 4 miles
he trudged beneath a marmalade sunrise
as that memory swung loose and free between him.
He was moving away from her, but going nowhere
his shoes still tied to that secret place;
bearing backwards against the commuter drive,
like chewing gum on the soles of his feet.

Floral

My outer lips are like a flower.
Opened up to your tongue
like an iris touching daylight.
Grew in the wetness
towards something higher.
This flower
in twelve shades of hot
or more.

My Mother's Old Coat #2

My mother's old coat is traumatised.
Inside the lining is puckered and torn
Making it impossible
For anyone to get an arm through

And there it is: the solution
To all my years of adolescent struggle
The owning of the fact that no one
no one
can take my mother's place

My Mother's Old Coat #5

In the nineties
you get less
for your money.

Even the money
is getting

smaller.

In the seventies
you got more for your coins

and when you'd spent up
at least you had a   in your pocket
                        hole

to show for it.

Immigrants / Alien nation

They packed their suitcases
and made for the boats,
travelled for days on end
not knowing
when they might see a spouse
or their children again

leaving the reliable goodness
of what they knew to be true
to search for shelter
in dark places
where *no blacks*
or dogs were allowed.

Forsaking how it felt, the hub of familiarity
they forged a high priced tunnel
through soot and snow
so we could be freer
and able to travel farther than they.
But of all the bad things
we have learnt from them
(cluttered living rooms, bad taste in furniture)
they never showed us the Uzi
or the drughole to hell
so what are we doing to ourselves,
who are we imitating
now?

SuAndi

Born in Manchester, in recent years I have become a travelling artist working mainly in North America. I do not write enough, I do not perform enough, but each and every day I am always an artist even when in my role as Cultural Director of artBlacklive (Black Arts Alliance). I have had an ICA (Keidan/Ugwu) Live Art Commission, *The Story of M*, which is still being booked four years on; and I was awarded a Winston Churchill Fellowship in 1996. Long chats with Kirk have taken my work to a different plane and too long telephone calls with friends and colleagues in Black Arts Alliance get me through each day.

Web Site: http://www.taliferro.com/artist/suandi/

Kirk

i'm pissed OK
i don't mean pissed
i mean pissed
like red wine grape
but pissed or not
i know he's good
you should hear, you should hear
you should hear him go
sort of sweet tones
low tones
high tones
graphic
you know graphic
he's painting with his tongue
licking descriptions
scenes i've never been
but i'm living it
liking it
doing it
you know
with him one to one
this is music and
if music be the food of life
brother play on
play on play on brother play on
and you know why i'm smiling
you can see i am smiling

he's doing that
drawing a grin on me
even when he's speaking low
and those young lips
move that way that is his
and you hear me sigh
and ummm, ummm,
with a smile
this is the man
too much boy in him
to be old enough to be creative
yet he's hurting me
paining me
caressing me
with his words
poetry
he speaks poetry

Southern

Sweat wrapped him in muskiness
that would have been sexy on a frame
thirty years younger
25 pounds heavier firmer
now it suggested stillness
like mothballs
on a suit worn only for funerals
occasionally a tear had the nerve
to free itself and begin a slow flow down his nose
then it would tether at the corner of his mouth
a vain attempt to moisten
lips cracked and bleeding
but he didn't weep
old yellow eyes seeming dead
concentrated on the way forward
looking down they saw only dirt
and they knew dirt in all its disguises
speeding up
his body moved easily
through a neighbourhood of no importance
to him - this day,
and when he reached her
his large hands southern
reached out with a tenderness
of a father who loves the touch of his daughter

Grace

sad now and longing to tell a story Grace settled
      herself easy into centre
space and inhaled to gather attention
held onto it in order to evoke tension for her tale
the slight movement of her head
hardly anything at all
yet a gigantic indication of her sufferance
then a hand fell from nowhere to indicate the
      finality of her state
in the night she whispered
causing her audience to lean towards her
in the stillness
when the fortunate sleep peaceful
the countdown of the day passing
and the expectation of the new
when birds shiver into being and night owls burp
      away their supper
so it begins
never open
my eyes capture details cinematic in technicolour
      and my awe is signified by
the stillness of my heart
i hear the city sleeping
far away from the sound that now prevails
and have to resist laughter at the ridiculousness of
      the situation i find myself awake to

you may wonder at my madness i do
i do so why not you
for you have always expressed a concern as to my
	state of mind
in daylight even at my most normal
i know that you have thought that i might not
	make it through
and it is true that every step is precarious
every moment dangerous
every action tempting an inevitable fate
and here i am now
living evidence of all your diagnosis
telling you that each night they come
wearing their chains
carrying the burden of their shackles
and asking
in the wail of one voice
for revenge
retribution
and i worry that in time
they will persuade me and i will come for your
	head as a token of all that has
been Babylon

The Witness

Mornings always too quick to dawn.
Even in the dark of winter they woke her.
Sitting she grins stretched lipped
and sighs for one hour, one day more.
But holding herself determined
she moves bladder tight across the hall.
Then sharp relief
inhaling at the same time
the scent of her own water.
Hungry cat and dirty dishes greet her
as now her speed up
she begins the beginning of her day wondering
if she needs to wash and groom her hair
or escape the chore for one day more.
Time flies and two hours pass before at last
she is ready.
The day holds no surprises
brown post of theatre flyers
no bills thank God and no pay either.
Still her credit is lousy but plastic and possible
and her cheques as durable as an old durex.
Today she moves elegantly from door to car
going nowhere
eager to arrive.
Today she tours old neighbourhoods
churning up childhood memories of a mother's love
sworn friendships of a lifetime that she grew out of.

Here she stalls the engine
corner sitting,
remembering kisses and hot hands
when a youth hits her vision
and her heart leaps into her mouth
an invisible red
pumping in unison with the wound in his head
And no one will ever believe
that she didn't hear the bullet –
see the car –
Remembers nothing only that
she witnessed death
and her heart refuses to recover.

Blue Eyes

Do you remember the sweat of her
the rise of her belly
as you reached to kiss her Venus
You journey through intimacies
sex-scraping pen across the page
so erotic lines come easily for you
but the dimpled thigh which you studied on
is no longer an image
Do you remember the sweat of her
Audiences squirm
squeezing buttocks of all proportions
as you expose each touch
but your mouth can no longer taste her breasts
nor see the face as she towers above you
Such writings are not personal you tell your critics
the poet breaks all rules for his art
still in rare moments when metaphors evade you
your nostrils swell searching for her on the air
In that final thrust
you rise
stomach solid in ecstasy
to kiss her mouth
and the fullness of her blue eyes
lock with yours
this is neither love nor hate
pleasure nor passion
and lust you define with the full stop of a verse

but her sweat lingers
somewhere behind your ear
on your eyebrow
somewhere where you cannot lick her away

Kiss

Who kissed you this morning
laid rich lips
ripe with loganberries
across your brow
to ease the pain
who saw lips puckered
to reveal a tongue
rasped with agony
then took a taste of you

Picture

someone painted a picture
of herself
but it had no face
it wasn't a painting but a photograph
of one arm suspended by nothing
held up by emptiness
in it there were many colours
all neutral
it was a black and white
the scenery was vast
and she had painted every detail
in wide white sweeps
the arm was a negative
so dark I could make out every pore of flesh
she called it 'me'
and I recognised myself.

Private and Silently

I need to go home to look at my pubes
check them
inspect them
Naturally they are with me now
but this task is too intricate for
hotel rooms
a friend's futon
(read glorified and thin put-down settee)
or even the most cosiest of spare rooms ready to
  meet every need
I need to see my pubes
My routine
not too elaborate
leg over armchair
mirror placed carefully on thigh
reading lamp angled
in private and silently
Even if I could afford cosmetology
no skill could remove the grey I find there
an increasing shroud to my wilting womanhood
and so
I pluck and cry
pluck and cry

Contemporary

I can't be
if I'm growing
I can't see
if I'm crying
I can't love
if I'm dying
and I'm dying

I can't win
if I'm losing
I can't cope
if I'm failing
I can't hope
if I'm dying
and I'm dying

I can't change
if it must be
I can't love you
if you hate me
I can't survive on misery
so leave me

I can't dream of tomorrow
when each day brings sorrow
this is why my laughter is hollow
I'm dying

Can't Get Out of Jail

this isn't monopoly living
before he was schooled full term
he had already doubled up, tripled up
4-manned himself into space time
shuffled a line like the old days
sat dog like in a corner and whimpered
ran fleet footed before tripping
and slammed again
doing months, doing months, doing doing time
no day different from tomorrow
no misery free from yesterday
stupid and walking like a zombie out on the street
searching for times long gone
brothers turning to dust since he last hung a block
feeling isolated in freedom
feeling scared in his own back yard
stumbling to make small words with those who
      breed him
and love him less now than before he lost the will
      to be
he telling tall stories of other guys lives
trying to build himself a reputation
and when people turn to get their shit together
the only way they know how
working, saving
he already planning a longer stay
a 6 to 9 or maybe 12 to 15

home
the brother wants to go home
to a regular place
where the key turns
and the door clanks
and the light don't ever go out
and monopoly is a reality for the brother
who can't get out of jail

Malcolm Roy Andi Assassin X, 1941-95

Tight as a fist
memory retains images of madness
corrupt days tempering intolerance
want and need competing

Torture forces fingers to spread
and reveal a space bright with colour
a coat hung on the wall
trousers over a lamp shade
and sunglasses worn by a book
unread and not needed
but literally digested.

Then anger or tears
and the fist closes
a hammerhead of strength
that no coaxing can relax

Sleep weakens
and laughter creeps out into the night
and smiles like full lunar
with all its insanity
now it is love time
and kisses flow as easy now as then

But grief wins over
and a tear like oil brings the dawn
and the light frightens the heart
making it flutter
and the hand of memory once again
rolls tight into a fist
to protect it from loss

Shamshad Khan

Born in Leeds, Yorkshire, I trained as a biologist. I first started writing in 1988. I have had poetry published in magazines and anthologies including *Flame* (Crocus Books), *The Fire People* (Payback Press), *Bitter Sweet* (Women's Press) and *Nailing Colours* (Crocus Books), have had a short story published with Virago and featured on Radio 4's *Love Thang*. My poetry performances have included deaf signing and collaborations with contemporary dancers and musicians.

Silver Threads

Together we built a palace
mahal
domes and minarets
tiny blue tiles and mirrors.

Wandered
hand in hand
warm feet
on cool floors.

Ran up stairs to call
from towers piercing skies.

Rushed through gardens
pomegranates and white flowers
ruby sweet pungent scent.

Trailed feet in fountained water
and when night fell
argued how many stars
embroidered the sky.

Sari like folds from the heavens
to drape us
liquid blue chiffon
and silver threads

we lay and unthreaded.
How rich we were
silver knots
untied piled high.

It was whilst i was lying thus
stars in my hands
and the heavens on my lap

that you left.
i searched amongst the reams
of translucent hope
fearing at first that you had been smothered

or like a baby
choked on a silver thing.

i searched our palace for years.
Until
no longer ours
it became mine

all hope lost
single voice ringing
echoes returned
thrown from wall to wall.

i gathered our treasures and hid them in my purse

silver bits
spangled love

proof that i had not dreamed alone.

Firstsound

Mother now i understand
the green clinical fear
of this land
fresh

and you held onto me
longer
than you needed

didn't release me

i must have sensed

turned my head away
feet first
appeared
when you agreed
we'd have to take it on

still
i wouldn't leave
your space
my place

so they pulled
forceps
and turned me

the first sound
i heard on my release
lying between your thighs

were your screams
and the second

His name (Allah-u-Akbhar)*

and your throbbing body wet
always untimely
the release.

* refers to the practice of reciting prayers in the ears of a new born
baby so the first sound it hears on entering the world is the name
of God.

Under the Arches

Under the arches
of my feet

you rest your head
your oil shaved scalp
warm

so the curve
of your head
fits

grips
the part

of my feet
that never touch the ground.

I wouldn't mind a free trip home

Yesterday, I was trying to park my car, except
three white boys, only just old enough to be driving
stood in the space I was moving into

they looked at me but just stood there.
Narrow minded nearly wide boys,
I edged further in
my metal machine finally forcing them out -
"don't fucking try or I'll send you back home."

My answer was shorter
and just as sweet:
"fuck off"

Later, I wondered whether that had been a free trip
        to Leeds
or Pakistan he had offered me.
If it had been the latter I thought
maybe I'd been hasty in my reply.

Spider Woman

She spun the argument
with a thread
he could not follow

perfecting
the delicate construction

until he
unsuspecting

fell
entangled

to
his

gentle destruction

Undoing symbols

His black velvet cap small
dome to cover the skull he knew
we would know straight away when we
uncurled the ringlets one on each side of his
     surprisingly white face
in that place in our minds
where we sit cross legged like the shoe maker's
     pixies
undo what we see
refuse to let things just be

Subconscious actions

She dropped the bowl of orange flowers
she thought smelt like roses should
blue glass, pebble beads
and water soaked her feet
it had not
unexpectedly fallen from her hands
but told her slowly before it disengaged itself
and slowly too had
fallen
gathered speed and exploded
ended
its blue life broken
it was no longer her favourite vase

heart (w)rap

i strap my heart
tightly
bind it strong

tough
was how i presented it to you

how you questioned me
on what was in this strange parcel

first tentatively
and then held it in your hands
and feeling the warmth
and faint beat
you guessed

and since
have tugged at the string
i so carefully bound
in protection

how you teased open
layer after layer
unravelled it all
until it lay open before you

how you were repulsed

when you saw
the pale blood drained flesh

i too drew back

hardly recognising the half healed mass
before us
disgusted by the scars
you did not ask
in what battle they were won

but fled

the faint hearted
i whispered to myself
won't inherit

and began again
to bind

Ms Havisham

His was a deep red
sweet blood
sticky kind of love
that damned spot
oceans could not erase

and the heady perfume of fear
overpowers.

I stagger light headed
towards the crimson screen
where Ms Havisham
still sits and waits.

Her wedding dress grey with dust
her guests still not arrived.

The groom she has resurrected
at the head of the table
lovers banquet
candles flickering
light and shadow
on her expectant face.

Her yellowed skin hangs
dull
half opened eyes

peer across the table's
lace landscape.

Cobwebs the spiders have deserted
drape the untouched feast.
The carcass of a pig
long dead
skeleton tent
vacated shelter.

She bears no mind
to the new life emerging
pink unopened eyes bulge warm
thin flesh around pea hard bellies
doesn't hear
the high pitched squeals
of mice

but smiles
red lipstick lips
politely
and passes the wine
to her hungry ghost guests.

Oppressed Coverage

You don't often give us a prime time slot

but make an exception
in times of trouble
when you star us on the news
on ITV **and** BBC

bomb blasts it was us who did it
famines the result of Islamic rule
demonstrations only of mindless masses
women covered it's got to be oppressive

and it won't be the last time there's confusion
about Muslims and Islam in this nation
whether on radio or TV
rampaging fundo oppressive repressives
you know
even I'm starting to get
a negative picture of me

bomb blasts it was us who did it
famines the result of Islamic rule
demonstrations only of mindless masses
women covered it's got to be oppressive

and whatever the news
you restate your views with such ease
always finishing with a call to prayer

any excuse to show us on our knees.

Outspoken

Umbrella stands discarded
limbs blown apart and skeleton exposed

inside out and skin unstitched
it must have been raining the day he left you

I imagine it must have been raining really hard and
        you pushed
against the beating
and the wind throbbed at you your chest bellowing
then ripped you apart and wretched
your ribs broken deflated lungs punctured
and no holding down could breathe life back into
        you
your body dishevelled
soaked skin clinging to
your disjointed frame

he left you leant against the wall
below the billboard picture
of a woman smiling too widely
it was raining on that day

Trudy Blake

I was born in Kingston, Jamaica and came to England in the Sixties. I worked as a packer in Salford factories and as a sewing machinist doing piecework. I have performed my poetry all over the North West, and have acted - in community plays, and as a television extra on Prime Suspect. I started to write poetry when I joined a local creative writing group.

This Woman Running In

Me joints them gone stiff
me starter won't start
me connections won't connect.
I need more than a magnet
to make my electricity flow

I need my engine to run on its own.
But don't care what I try, me joints
won't tighten up. I need a 100% replacement.
I'm a total wreck!

My Baby Father

He got up, had a shower,
fill up his belly with me
ackee and saltfish, fry
dumplin and cocoa tea.

He was so full that he
stretch and belch. Then he
put on his best suit. As
he start walking through
the door, I asked him

You a go somewhere man?
Said he was going for a job.
I sit on the chair and watch
the man go out. He look so
handsome that it make my heart
beat fast.

About eleven o'clock I see
Miss Lue Lue, a run come,
so I asked,
-what wrong Miss Lue Lue,
somebody dead?

-I come to tell you that
you man a married a strange
woman out a Wesley church.

Ka-Ka!

I couldn't believe me earhole.
I nearly drop dead, the man sleep
here last night, whisper his babblings
into my ears, now I hear the
son-of-a-bitch a marry someone else!

I stand at the corner of the street
thinking, what to do?
The man drive pass me later
with his new wife. She look
so cocky. Hope she break
his ass.

Lover Boy

It was seven o'clock,
he went out driving:
to see my brother
for an hour or two.
He didn't come back
till after midnight.

Lost my bearings, he said
went round and round and round.
I didn't believe him,
this man of excuses.
He invent them as
he goes along.

Last time, I caught him red handed
with a woman hot on his tracks.
Said she was his brother woman.
But if I believe that, I'll
believe anything.

Another time, two women were fighting over him.
One lock herself inside his house,
the other outside looking in.
He stood there, laughing.

He is a ladies' man,
a liar, a trickster.

But he can charm the pants
off a woman. He's a bad boy.
But so, so lovable.

The Grass

I said to my other half:
    how about it -
are you going to get
your ass out there and
cut the grass?
Pardon me?
was his reply.

Let pardon be damned
are you cutting the grass
or what?

Or what, he said.

Girl Indoors

Can't you fine something to
do, girl? my mother call out.
The music was playing and
I can't stand still

I look through the window.
Girls walking up and down
with their boy friends and
I have to be inside working

I cook, all day I clean
and sew. What more can she
want me to do? I'm just waiting
for night to come so that
I can be out there with my man,
hugging, kissing,
talking soft.

Father

He came, he saw me
and then he said *behave you self girl,*
I hear you giving you mother trouble.
Never seen this man for years,
says he is my father.

My mother buy me a dress
she say *mourn for you father.*
Now this dead man a tell me
behave you self gal.
Last I heard from him he went
to live in the country town:
going back to farming, he said,
city life no good for me.
Another woman was his wife.

My mother struggle to bring me up
can't live on air pie
and his name alone.

Lord things really hard sometime
not easy for a woman on her own.
Now here is this stranger,
my father, telling me what to do.

Take Away That Brochure

I'll wear short skirts
if I want to - that
don't make me stupid.

I'll have a tot of rum
to warm my bones
step out to the disco
and do my rubber chicken dance.

So don't buy me granny slippers,
I won't wear them. And take away
that brochure for the retirement home.

A rarity

Looking for a man
I can trust
One that don't go screwing
around the minute I turn
my back

He can look at other women
but not touch
He's got to keep his hands
for me, that's
what I want. This man
is a rarity.

Winter

Withered
from the frost
brown leaves
drop silently
to the ground

A chill wind
fused my bones.

Under the Mango Tree

Under the mango tree
we sit and eat and eat and eat
till our bellies full
Then we filled our baskets
and walked up the road.

Tang Lin

Born in Yung Shu Au - a small village in the New Territories in the shadow of Hong Kong, I came to Britain in 1972. I trained as a painter in Sunderland and in Syracuse, New York. My main literary influence is the T'ang dynasty poems. I use images from nature to describe the emotional and spiritual levels of beauty and suffering. I try to combine the tranquility I find in Buddhism with the turbulence of everyday living.

naked frame

I

as if walking
on a lake that is calm
the heart
            still

surrendering
to the river of life

II

starry starry   sky
magic of fantasy and dreams

the wind kisses the stillness
        mist descends upon the earth

i sit on the balcony
and gaze

through a rustic and naked frame
a red rose bathing in the moonlight
erupting
        my sky of dreams

in the shadows
        the river flows tears

i sit on the balcony
        and gaze at my own thoughts

        chanting in the surreal
            light

i travelled
12,000 miles
to find myself sitting with my shadow
a blue wind
haunts me
as i sit on this balcony
in somebody else's house

III

a blindfolded child dancing, singing
  what is life
  who is me
  again and again and again...

whispering
  in the wind
    flowers

the wings
  of butterflies
    the loneliness of words

time becomes timeless
  wind flowers

time becomes timeless
  wind flowers moon

where are we now
    wind flowers moon

withering in my dream
  petals of a pink tulip

a woman
     sitting on a rock
          waiting

IV

you touch me
      you kiss me
      you make love to me

water
      floods
            the earth
i hear the song of love
            in the wind

the grass
      drinks the rain
i hear the song of love
            in the wind

the wind
      is
      singing

the song of love
            is in the wind

V

in solitude
    there is sundown
        moonrise

    the autumn wind
    brushing

last night
    the rain fell softly
    massaged
    the earth

now this morning
    spring birds
    chant - speak
    gentle waves

i am woken
    not by the rain
    nor by the chanting
but
by the brightness of dawn
and with a wandering thought:
    where is the chinese moon

VI

you bring
a basket of plants
i see yesterday's guilt
      hidden in the shadow of your eyes

dunkery beacon*
lies in silence waiting for new autumn

wind blowing
      the emptiness
the rain rustling
      the blues

*the highest point on Exmoor, Devon.

VII

i will
kiss your lips
     like the spring kisses the earth
i will touch you
     like the wind caresses trees

VIII

we lovers
    standing in the rain
    watching, listening
to the ocean

whichever way we turn
    we see death
    we should not be surprised
    illness
    ageing, death
        are the confirmation of life

        rising and falling
        rising and falling

    the ocean hushes
    its waves
    rising and falling
    rising and falling
    softly

the stillness of rock
    beautiful
    infinity beautiful

IX

against the whiteness
        i stand
        nowhere is
        and everywhere is

silently
      in the shape of love
         the snow is
            falling

Seni Seneviratne

I was born in Yorkshire in 1951, saved from a drowning birth by the cold steel of surgical knives. My mother was English, gave me her voice and her wicked laugh. My father was Sri Lankan, gave me my blackness, a love of writing and his unspoken memories to discover. I have learned to cherish all my roots and now I am blossoming. I am a writer, singer, photographer and performer, and have been published in various anthologies and on tape.

My Father's Half-Told Story

Looking through the mist
I see him twelve years old
wipe confusion from his eyes
they are deep brown, questions
piercing the freezing haze
of a colourless winter
wondering where the green disappears
in the strange cobbled streets
asking why his father went
and why his mother died.

He sailed on the Orama
across the Indian Ocean
savoured the last taste
of the mango sunsets
of Sri Lanka
lost his tears
in sharp sea spray
found his mother
in a dream of home
locked her in his heart
with the keys of a religion
which had travelled East from Portugal
four hundred years before.

He sailed beyond Portugal
saw his mother rise

from the waters of
the Indian and Atlantic Oceans
and promise to stay with him
a memory sweeter than her songs
He brought his white gods
home to England's winter
where the skies like dirty blankets
covered people with frozen smiles
who had no rice flour or rickshaws
and burnt black rocks
to keep them warm.

He saw his father marry
a white child-bride
sail back to the East
Left him dreaming of
ocean liners and Colombo streets
Left him in exchange
with a white girl's parents
Left him to become
the odd-boy-out
the black face in the school photo
the curiosity
holding onto his religion
as a passport to acceptance.

Looking through the mist
I find his puzzled face
reflecting mine scouring the years

for my own hazy history
sepia photos, silken saris
and half-told stories
But I can't see far enough
never asked the questions
to know how he lived
through so many losses and leavings.

Beneath the Waterfall

A tall black woman came to me the first night
haunting my dreams with her smile
and I knew the house was full of spirits

These days have stretched my tired mind
like a roll of white paper
The words fall over me like droplets
I'm crouching beneath the waterfall
savouring the sound

Wrapped in an Indian shawl
I have toasted crumpets on an open fire
caressed your taste buds with coconut dahl
strained to link my mixed-up past with yours
ghosts and vampires of childhood nightmares
became the loupgarou and soucouyant
that we wove our stories around
And one night I caught a glimpse
of my Sri Lankan father
in the face of a Caribbean poet
saw Asia melt into Africa

Each night I bathe in rosemary oil
next day trawl my mind for images

Purple Heart

I am lazy as the Zambesi
drifting, treading water
just round the corner
maybe there'll be
the rushing
       roaring
             falling
the juice of the mango
to curl my tongue round.
My heart has grown
purple with longing
but July comes and goes
each year and still
no lover paints
her pleasure on my skin.

Some nights she comes
and seasons my dreams
finds me in Colombo streets
leaves the print of her hand
in my palm
the curve of her skin
on my back
the breath of her kiss
on my neck
but always her face
escapes me

When morning comes
I bathe in the memories
and drift on
lazy waiting.

Jasmine Memories

We met like two oceans
asked the breaking
waves cautious questions
drifted into easy days
fingering the smell of
growing passion
running wild
against the storms
looking for shadows
in the sand

when I left the sky
was blood orange
tearing me away
from you

now I eat your words
for breakfast after
night-time travels
where I find you sleeping
under the mountain
dazzle your eyes
with shining seaweed
and burst my banks to
drench your dreams
in jasmine memories
too strong to fade

For Kate

Roses shout above
a table filled with
red remembering
fragrant years of growing
full of pains and pleasures
under my watchful eyes
now you dance out of my reach
a rainbow arched to freedom
a woman from my blood
tasting your own choices
popping with passion
glowing in the heat
of future plans
wanting more
leaving my nest

I remember the velvet
of your luscious
baby skin born on
a silent morning
coaxed to cry
blue feet turning pink
now red celebrates
your arrival at
the door of tomorrow

blood red drowning

blood red drowning
they cut my mother
saved our lives
in a sudden blast
of light and cold air

hungry for warmth
I craved skin
was cradled
in empty space
under a glass quilt

In her dream
a pink blanket
her baby's shroud
blood-stained prayers
too late to save

miracle survival
grandma's candles
father's prayers
soothed my mother's
buried fears

her feelings sewn
behind the scars
she never found

a way to tell
except the blame

mine were mute
wanted, nearly lost
rejected, over protected
hero and villain
of family stories

I carried it all
wrapped in tight bundles
around my back
crying for comfort
rocked to fitful sleep

never made it up
to her who never
made it up to me
who both never needed
to make anything up

only to accept
this pain
blood red
in which
we drowned

year of winters

the cold front came
in our year of winters
took away my friend
left me grieving
in dream gardens
full of red rose trees
we made fires
licked flames of desire
plaited new memories
with old ones
gathered blue roses
in early mornings
promised ourselves
a year of summers

Memoried Mosaic

In the circle
of our faces
the history of the world
unfolds its
memoried mosaics
at our feet
dispersed travellers
on forced journeys
workers, wars and weddings
intermingling continents
and cultures

We are the lines
of connection
crossing boundaries
of nationalism
unwinding
intricate roots
redrawing the map
of imperialism
in flesh and blood
colours

the colour of her eyes

a year passes
memories crowd
into spaces

can't remember
the colour of her eyes
found her in yellow
trying to shine
but the light in
her eyes had wilted

can't

saw grey cancer's
rigid corset
suck the sparkle
from her eyes
scrape the song
from her voice
break her wings

remember

pushed her
into the sunshine
wrapped in thick
dark clothes to cover

.

her regrets nothing
to cover mine raw
in the yellow heat

the colour

watched her float
away a slow bubble
out of reach
translucent skin
reflecting rainbows
couldn't catch
the sparkle

of her eyes

a year passes
tight tears seal mine
unpicking memories
falling apart

Lena Rulak

Who are you Lena Rulak
mother of my father
daughter of a lawyer
Eurasian Burgher
of Sri Lanka?

You are my father's
speechless memories
moving through me
like the sea
in my restless sleep

you wrap me in his body
clothe me in words
that have wandered
through oceans
wash me up
on the dream tide

your arms are wide
and change the blue
to gold
you treasure me
in smells
of spices and kindness
cradle me
in a language
I never knew
turn my questions
into songs

Cinnamon Roots

Cinnamon sweet wood spice
once traded like gold
when I look for my roots
I find you yellowish brown
like my winter skin
native of Sri Lanka
growing wild in the jungles
of the Kandy Highlands

1492 Columbus never finds you
sailing westwards to the lands
of the Arawak Indians
he promises spices and gold
trophies for a Spanish Queen
brings her Taino slaves as 'gifts'

But Portugal travels East
to an island that falls like
a teardrop from the tip of India
finds your soft sweetness
wraps it in hard cash
grows rich on your rarity
founding a spice trade
that deals in blood

The Dutch make plantations
tame your wild fragrance

that can never sweeten their breath
demand quotas of your bark
enforced by death and torture
burn down your August harvest
fabled fuel of the phoenix fire
to keep up the prices

Dutch East India
becomes British East India
your acres grow in the rain
and heat of Sri Lanka
filling the coffers
of the British Empire

1992 I buy your ground aroma
in pre-packed jars fry you
with aubergines and coriander
look for my roots
find you yellowish brown
like my winter skin
native of Sri Lanka
growing wild in the jungles
of the Kandy Highlands

ORDER FORM

TITLE	QTY	PRICE
Nailing Colours		£7.50
Dim Sum		£6.95
No Limits		£6.50
Looking for Trouble		£5.95
Crocus Five Women Poets		£5.95
Other Crocus Titles		
The Delicious Lie		£4.95
Flame		£4.50
Talkers Through Dream Doors		£3.50
Black and Priceless		£3.50
Holding Out		£3.50

TOTAL _____

Please send a cheque or postal order, made payable to Commonword Ltd., covering the purchase price plus 75p per book postage and packing.

NAME_____

ADDRESS_____

_____

_____POSTCODE_____

Please return to: **Commonword, Cheetwood House, 21 Newton Street, Manchester M1 1FZ**